Space

Astronauts

Charlotte Guillain

www.raintreepublishers.co.uk
Visit our website to find out
more information about
Raintree books.

To order:

☎ Phone 0845 6044371

🖹 Fax +44 (0) 1865 312263

🖥 Email myorders@capstonepub.co.uk

Customers from outside the UK please telephone +44 1865 312262

Raintree is an imprint of Capstone Global Library Limited, a company
incorporated in England and Wales having its registered office at 7 Pilgrim
Street, London, EC4V 6LB – Registered company number: 6695582

Raintree is a registered trademark of Pearson Education Limited, under
licence to Capstone Global Library Limited

Text © Capstone Global Library Limited 2009
First published in hardback in 2009
Paperback edition first published in 2010
The moral rights of the proprietor have been asserted.

Edited by Sian Smith, Rebecca Rissman, and Charlotte Guillain
Designed by Joanna Hinton-Malivoire
Picture research by Tracy Cummins and Heather Mauldin
Production by Duncan Gilbert
Originated by Heinemann Libray
Printed and bound in China by South China Printing
Company Ltd

ISBN 978 0 431 02047 1 (hardback)
13 12 11 10 09
10 9 8 7 6 5 4 3 2 1

ISBN 978 0 431 02054 9 (paperback)
14 13 12 11 10
10 9 8 7 6 5 4 3 2 1

British Library Cataloguing in Publication Data
Guillain, Charlotte
  Astronauts. - (Space)
  1. Astronauts - Juvenile literature 2. Manned space flight
  - Juvenile literature
  I. Title
  629.4'5

Acknowledgements
We would like to thank the following for permission to reproduce
photographs: AP Photo pp.**16**, **22** (©Pat Sullivan); Getty Images pp.**6**,
11 (©NASA) **15**, **17** (©Space Frontiers/Stringer), **18** (©Stockbyte);
NASA pp.**9** (©GRIN/James McDivitt), **10**, **14** (©GRIN), **19** (©National
Aeronautic and Space Administration/Human Space Flight), **20**
(©GRIN/Charles M. Duke Jr.), **23a**, **23b** (©GRIN), **23c** (©National
Aeronautic and Space Administration/Human Space Flight); Photo
Researchers p.**21** (©Science Source); Photo Researchers Inc. pp.**4**
(©Pekka Parviainen), **5** (©Science Source/NASA), **13** (©Science Source);
Reuters p.**12** (©NASA); Reuters p.**12** (©NASA); ©UPI pp.**7**, **8**.

Front cover photograph reproduced with permission of NASA (©James
McDivitt). Back cover photograph reproduced with permission of NASA
(©GRIN/Charles M. Duke Jr.).

Every effort has been made to contact copyright holders of material
reproduced in this book. Any omissions will be rectified in subsequent
printings if notice is given to the publishers.

Contents

Space

Space is up above the sky.

People can travel into space.

Astronauts

People who travel into space are called astronauts.

Astronauts learn about space.

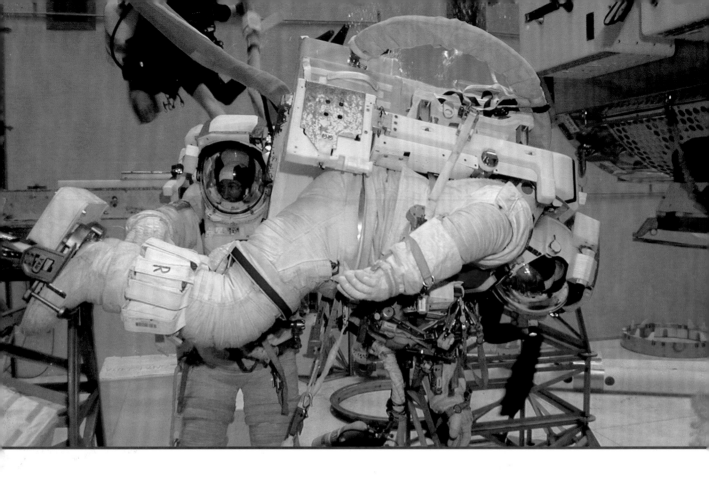

Astronauts learn to work in water.

This is like working in space.

space shuttle

Astronauts travel in a space shuttle.

The space shuttle takes astronauts into space.

Astronauts can see Earth from space.

Astronauts float in space.

Astronauts wear a special suit
in space.

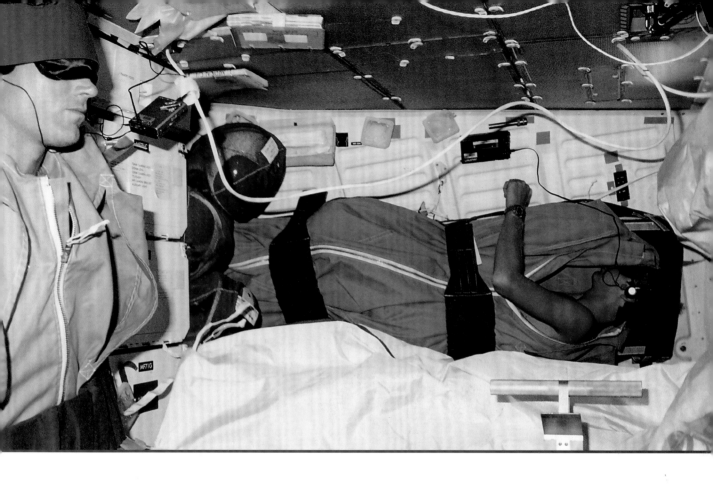

Astronauts sleep in a special bed
in space.

Astronauts have special food in space.

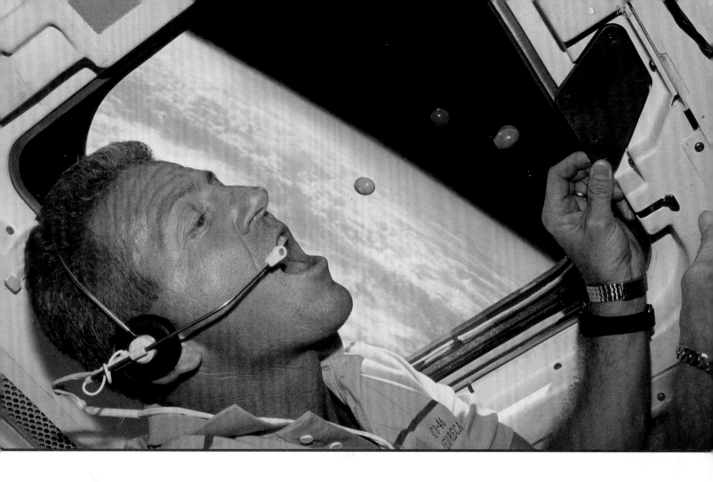

Food floats in space.

The space station

Astronauts are building a space station in space.

Astronauts live on the space station.

The Moon

Astronauts have visited the Moon.

They brought Moon rocks and dust
back to Earth.

Can you remember?

What is this?

Answer on p.24

Picture glossary

 **astronaut** person who travels into space

 **space shuttle** vehicle people use to travel into space

 **space station** a place built in space where people can live

Index

Answer to question on p.22: Food that can be eaten in space.

Notes for parents and teachers
Before reading
Ask the children if they know what an astronaut is. Have they ever seen any programmes about astronauts on the television? What sort of clothes do astronauts wear? If they were an astronaut where would they like to visit?

After reading
• Make astronauts. Help children to draw round each other on large sheets of paper and cut out the shape. Use white or silver paint for the suit and coloured circles for the controls on the suit. Attach two plastic bottles to the back to represent the oxygen tanks. Suspend the astronauts from the ceiling or around the walls.

• Role play. Tell children that they are going to be astronauts and visit the planets. Tell them to put on their space suits and check they have their breathing apparatus. Take off in the space shuttle and visit Mars. Tell the children that it is very hot during the day but freezing cold at night. Look at all the red rocks and the enormous volcano. Continue visiting other planets before you finally decide to return to Earth.